days

WITH
THE
MASTER
FISHERMAN

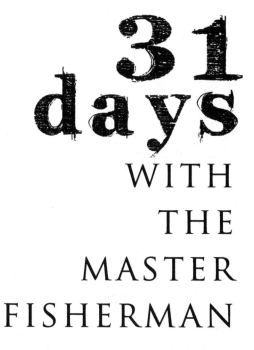

31 days

WITH THE MASTER FISHERMAN

A DAILY DEVOTIONAL ON
BRINGING CHRIST TO OTHERS

R. LARRY MOYER

Kregel
Publications

31 Days with the Master Fisherman: A Daily Devotional on Bringing Christ to Others

© 1997 by EvanTell, Inc.

Published by Kregel Publications, a division of Kregel, Inc., P.O. Box 2607, Grand Rapids, MI 49501.

Library of Congress Cataloging-in-Publication Data
Moyer, R. Larry
   Thirty-one days with the master fisherman: a daily devotional on bringing Christ to others / R. Larry Moyer.
       p.   cm.
   1. Witness bearing (Christianity)—Meditations. 2. Evangelistic work—Meditations. 3. Devotional calendars.
I. Title.
BV4520.M68   1997   248'.5—dc20   96-29404
                                                                                        CIP

ISBN 978-0-8254-3569-0

Printed in the United States of America
09 10 11 12 13 / 5 4 3 2 1

To my many brothers and sisters in Christ throughout the world who have constantly encouraged me to write on the pages of a book what God had already written on the pages of my heart. I am forever in debt to you for the unending inspiration you have been to me. May this book be a small deposit on the tremendous debt I owe you.

Contents

Introduction / 9

1. Special Privileges / 11

2. Please Keep It Simple / 13

3. Danger: Live Tongue / 15

4. "It Isn't Gonna Do Any Good" / 18

5. Reaching Relatives / 20

6. Every Minute Counts / 23

7. Needed: A Door of Opportunity / 26

8. Get Ready! Get Set! / 29

9. It's Just Plain Scary! / 32

10. With Whom Are You Trying to
    Impress Them? / 35

11. Lord, Increase the Tribe / 37

12. When All Else Fails, Just Follow / 40

13. Die Later—but Decide Now! / 43

14. I Don't Enjoy Non-Christians / 45

15. The Proper Fear in Evangelism / 48

16. Kind to Whom? You Must Be Kidding! / 50

17. Is Your Life an Illustration? / 53

18. Teamwork / 56

19. Having a Problem with Patience? / 59

20. Too Good to Keep to Ourselves / 62

21. The Right Kind of Preoccupation / 65

22. Dare to Be Different! / 68

23. Basic Football / 71

24. Good-bye, Guilt Trip / 73

25. Living Life Backwards? / 75

26. Beyond Your Greatest Imagination / 78

27. Wait Until You Hear This! / 81

28. Beam It Out / 84

29. Not Plus . . . Period! / 87

30. Given Anyone an Appetite Lately? / 90

31. No "Maybes" About It / 92

Introduction

Soon after I started full-time evangelism, I was asked to speak at a youth camp. Wanting to help young people in areas where we all struggle, I prepared a talk on the mind. I dug into the Scriptures with the question, "What does the Bible say about the mind?"

That study had a lasting impact in my life. I concluded that what the Bible said about our minds could be summarized in one sentence: What you dwell on in your mind, you produce with your life. Suddenly, I understood as never before why God tells us to meditate on the Scriptures. In Psalm 1, God describes a happy man by saying, "His delight is in the law of the Lord, and in His law he meditates day and night" (v. 2). What I dwell on in my mind, I produce with my life. The psalmist continues, "He shall be like a tree planted by the rivers of water, that brings forth its fruit in its season" (v. 3).

The same is true of evangelism. If you meditate on evangelism, you will reach out and evangelize. I've written this devotional for my brothers and sisters in Christ who are saying, "I want the Lord to use my life to populate heaven." I share numerous Scriptures and thoughts God has used to encourage me to let my life be an outreach to the lost. I'm an evangelist, but I have the same struggles in evangelism as everyone else. These verses, thoughts, and ideas have helped me overcome my fear of evangelism instead of allowing that fear to overcome me.

As you meditate on these devotionals about Jesus, the Master Fisherman, my prayer is that your life will be marked by consistency in evangelism. After all, what you dwell on in your mind, you produce with your life. Enjoy meditating! Enjoy evangelizing!

R. LARRY MOYER

1

Special Privileges

To read

> *But as we have been approved by God to be en-*
> *trusted with the gospel, even so we speak, not as*
> *pleasing men, but God who tests our hearts*
> (1 Thessalonians 2:4).

To consider

The apostle Paul never seemed to get the message that evangelism is supposed to be a pain, not a privilege, right? NOT!

The meaning behind Paul's words is that God examined Paul before giving him the Gospel, and God is still examining him today. With that in mind, Paul speaks as one who has the right message, has been told to spread it, and wants to please God. What others thought of Paul's message did not matter; what God thought was all that mattered.

Think of the ramifications of this knowledge in our personal evangelism. If we have the confidence that we are God's messengers sent out to spread the Good News, this knowledge affects our attitudes. We become keenly aware that if a lost person does not hear the Gospel from us, the next person who speaks to them could be someone spreading the *wrong* message. If they don't hear it from us, they may not hear anything at all! We are the individuals God entrusted with the message. What an honor, calling, and compliment that God would let us share His love with others. He could have chosen any way He wanted to get the Word out. Instead, He decided to entrust it to us.

To illustrate

The story is told of a man who was waiting by a shopping mall for his wife when an individual approached him and began a conversation. The stranger turned the conversation to spiritual things and asked the man, "Do you know if you're going to heaven?"

When the man's wife returned, the couple walked toward their car and she asked, "What did that man want?" "He wanted to know if I knew I was going to heaven." The wife responded, "That's none of his business!" "That's interesting," he answered. "If you had seen the expression on his face and heard the way he asked, you would have thought it was."

To meditate

God is bringing lost people to Christ. He simply wants to know if you'd like to be in on the action.

To pray

Have you let negative attitudes creep into your life as you contemplate evangelizing? Confess them to God, ask for His forgiveness, and begin today to see introducing non-Christians to Christ as a blessing, not a burden.

2

Please Keep It Simple

To read

> *For I delivered to you first of all that which I also received: that Christ died for our sins according to the Scriptures, and that He was buried, and that He rose again the third day according to the Scriptures, and that He was seen by Cephas, then by the twelve* (1 Corinthians 15:3–5).

To consider

We live in a world of conflicting messages. Health magazines warn us to get more exercise. Sports stadiums advertise their events by broadcasting, "Come early and park close. Avoid a long walk." One medical ad warned of the danger found in the yolk of the egg. An article in a medical journal insists that the warning about the yolk is a joke.

When it comes to the most important message—the Gospel—there should be no confusion. Paul states, "I delivered to you . . . what I also received." In Galatians 1:12, Paul explains that he did not receive the message from other people but from God. That message centers around four things that all concern Christ. (1) Christ *died* for our sins according to the Scriptures; (2) Christ was *buried;* (3) Christ *rose* again on the third day according to the Scriptures; and (4) Christ was *seen.*

His burial is proof that He died. The fact that He was seen is proof that He arose. This is the Gospel: Christ died for our sins and rose from the dead.

Why do we often make the message more difficult? Could it be that we begin to share more about the Bible and less about the Gospel? We begin to talk to lost people about how to *live* the Christian life before we've explained how to *enter* it. Could it be that we often forget the real message? A person lost in sin needs to hear the Good News of Christ— Christ died for our sins and rose from the dead.

To illustrate

During the 1960 Olympics, the *Saturday Evening Post* carried a cartoon picturing the winner of an ancient marathon. The messenger of victory stumbles, falling prostrate before the king in a palace. Suddenly, a puzzled look appears on his face and he blurts out, "I've forgotten the message."

To meditate

The Bible contains sixty-six books, but the Gospel contains just ten words—Christ died for our sins and rose from the dead.

To pray

As you have opportunities to present the Good News, ask God to help you present it as the apostle Paul did—clearly and simply.

3

Danger: Live Tongue

To read

"Their throat is an open tomb; With their tongues they have practiced deceit;" "The poison of asps is under their lips;" "Whose mouth is full of cursing and bitterness" (Romans 3:13–14).

To consider

If you ever wonder whether or not people are really depraved, just examine the above Scripture which explains human depravity in harsh language.

An "open tomb" refers to an individual being placed in a grave without an embalming process. If you were to dig up a grave a few days after someone was buried, the stench would knock you off your feet. The poison of asps mentioned in this Scripture refers to the Egyptian cobra snake. The cobra is extremely poisonous because there is a small sack that holds all its poison underneath its tongue.

We have been so affected by sin that, apart from the grace of God, everything that comes from our mouth is like the stench of an open grave; it's like the poison of a snake. That's why it's so much easier to point out someone's bad traits when you've only known them a short time. Our mouths are so full of cursing and bitterness that four-letter words are the predominant vocabulary of some people. Many non-Christians would rather not digest the Good News; they'd rather chew us out for sharing it.

What a change after we come to Christ! The same tongue that was an instrument of evil becomes an instrument of good. Through the ministry of the Holy Spirit the tongue that used to control us can now be controlled *by* us. What better way is there to use the tongue than to broadcast the message of Christ's death and resurrection?

To illustrate

As an elderly speaker was giving his message, the engineer in the sound booth was frustrated with how long it was taking the speaker to get to the point of his message. So the engineer whispered to himself, "Well, go ahead, you old goat." He failed to realize that his own microphone was turned on. Therefore, his words were not only to himself, but to the speaker and the audience of thousands of people. What potential the tongue has to damage! If it has such potential to hurt and destroy, think of the potential it has to do good. One person brought to Christ might lead another to Christ because of the process God started with the use of your tongue.

To meditate

Each day you make the decision whether your tongue will be a weapon for Satan or a witness for the Savior.

To pray

Have you ever thanked God for delivering you from the destructive power of your tongue? Have you thanked Him for the new way it can now be used to bear eternal fruit? Ask God to use your tongue this month to share with at least one person the grace of God as seen in His death and resurrection.

4

"It Isn't Gonna Do Any Good"

To read

Now when He had stopped speaking, He said to Simon, "Launch out into the deep and let down your nets for a catch." But Simon answered and said to Him, "Master, we have toiled all night and caught nothing; nevertheless at Your word I will let down the net." And when they had done this, they caught a great number of fish, and their net was breaking (Luke 5:4–6).

To consider

Those who have fished in the Sea of Galilee will tell you that fish come to the surface at night, but during the day the fish go down to the deep waters. Therefore, Christ's instructions to let down their nets for a catch, when they caught no fish during the night, must have made them wonder what Jesus was thinking.

I often wonder what *they* were thinking. "Have you forgotten the basic rules of fishing? Don't you understand how tired we are? Surely you realize it's not going to do any good."

Peter, most likely the master of the ship and the leader of the fishing company, understood something very simple. When Jesus speaks, the first rule is to *listen*. The verses explain the result of listening to Jesus' advice—they took in a net-breaking, boat-sinking load of fish.

What about you and me? When we sense that God wants us to evangelize, do we follow the example set by a listening Peter, or do we let excuses distract us from obedience to Christ's command?

To illustrate

During the Civil War General Lee sent word to Stonewall Jackson, explaining that the next time he rode in the direction of headquarters, he'd like to see him on a matter of no great importance.

The next morning Stonewall Jackson saddled his horse and against a wind of storm and snow, rode eight miles to General Lee's headquarters. General Lee was just finishing his breakfast and expressed his surprise that he had come so quickly through such a storm. General Jackson responded, "But you said that you wished to see me. General Lee's slightest wish is a supreme command to me."

To meditate

In speaking to others about the Good News of Jesus Christ, God's greatest need is always your obedience, not your opinion.

To pray

Ask God to make you obedient in sharing the Gospel. Be specific about excuses you often give, and ask Him to help you not let those excuses hinder your obedience.

5

Reaching Relatives

To read

Do not think that I came to bring peace on earth. I did not come to bring peace but a sword. For I have come to "set a man against his father, a daughter against her mother, and a daughter-in-law against her mother-in-law." And "a man's foes will be those of his own household" (Matthew 10:34–36).

To consider

After we receive God's gift of eternal life, graciously provided by Christ's death on the cross, God then looks at each of us and says, "Will you become my disciple?" He may use you as a plumber, or He may use you as a preacher. He may use you as an executive secretary or a store clerk. No matter where you are, He wants you to introduce people to Christ. As you do, your greatest struggles will often be with those who live in the same house with you.

In Matthew 10:34–36, He refers specifically to the tension that develops between a son and his father, a daughter and her mother, and a daughter-in-law and her mother-in-law. To those examples many more could be added. Why does it seem like everybody will listen to us except those in our own families?

I can think of two reasons. (1) They know us too well. They wonder what we could possibly have to share with them after the headaches and heartaches we gave them before we came to Christ. (2) Regardless of how lovingly we present the salvation of the Savior, they perceive that we are saying, "You blew it. In the most important area of life, the spiritual, you never gave *me* the message I so desperately needed to hear." Instead of thanking the Lord that you received the message and wanted to share it with them, they are intimidated.

For such people, someone outside the family can often do more than someone inside. The family member we are trying to reach will often listen to someone else bearing the same message simply because that person is not part of the family. We ought to do all we can to try and reach family members. Doing all we can includes praying that God will send someone in addition to us to speak to them.

To illustrate

A Jewish individual who came to Christ shared his new relationship with his parents. He later received the following letter from them. Objecting to his new-found faith, they wrote: "We have never met your wife. We have never met your children. You have never talked to us. You will never see us again, now or in heaven." Suppose God brings someone else into their lives to speak the Gospel to them. They have no basis upon which to express the same resistance. This simple fact may cause them to open up, not clam up.

To meditate

In reaching out to relatives, God might want to use you to start the conversation and have someone else finish it.

To pray

Think of a specific relative you want to see come to Christ. Now ask God to send someone in *addition* to you (not *instead* of you) to speak to them.

6

Every Minute Counts

To read

Walk in wisdom toward those who are outside, redeeming the time (Colossians 4:5).

To consider

No one understands better than an evangelist, who has interacted with many non-Christians, the need for a walk that backs up your talk. When non-Christians see a life that portrays Christ behind lips that present Him, the witness for the Savior becomes most powerful and productive.

As Paul wrote to the Colossians, that consistency is undoubtedly one of the reasons he admonished them to "walk in wisdom." He was not merely referring to their procedure in getting to the breakfast table in the morning but to their lifestyle during every hour of the day. "Redeeming the time" drives the point home. It means literally "buying up the opportunity." Each moment of your life is to be looked upon as an opportunity to live in a way that brings others closer to the cross, not farther away from it.

Our actions should always support what we say

and never detract from it. Whether it be the good deeds we do for a neighbor, the kindness we extend to a friend, the way we return love for anger, or our ability to be gentle when others are harsh, we ought to live in such a way that others have reason to say, "If that's Christianity, I want it." If we live in this meaningful way, we make every minute count for eternity—for those we speak the Gospel to, as well as for those to whom we show what a difference God has made in our lives.

If they want to see a good example of a Christian, they should not have to look beyond us. Our lives should make non-Christians want to tune in, not tune out.

To illustrate

A man who was antagonistic to Christ for years attributed his conversion to a timid neighbor. When the neighbor found out the impact he had had on this man's life, he was surprised. He explained, "I never spoke to you about Christ the way I should have."

The man answered, "No, you didn't. But you lived me to death. I could refute others' arguments and upset their logic, but I could not refute the way you lived."

To meditate

Since others are watching you live your life, for the sake of Christ, you need to watch the life you live.

To pray

Are there areas of your life that are hindering your witness? Confess those to God as sin and remove them from your life. Then ask God to use your life at home, at work, and every situation to make Jesus Christ attractive to people.

7

Needed: A Door of Opportunity

To read

> *Meanwhile praying also for us, that God would open to us a door for the word, to speak the mystery of Christ, for which I am also in chains, that I may make it manifest, as I ought to speak* (Colossians 4:3–4).

To consider

"It is so difficult to get him into spiritual things. The opportunity is never there." "We talk about everything under the sun, but I never get the chance to talk about spiritual things." "If I even allude to religious matters, she changes the subject."

The way to turn a conversation to spiritual things is more simple than we might realize. It begins with prayer. The apostle Paul's advice is, "Ask God for an open door." As a prisoner of the Roman empire, most likely handcuffed to a soldier twenty-four hours a day, Paul had opportunity to present Christ in prison. If I were a non-Christian Roman guard, the last thing I would wish is to be chained to the apostle Paul for twenty-four hours a day! Not wishing to be limited to the walls of a prison, Paul had a simple prayer request on behalf of himself and his associates—for God to open a door for the Word. Paul added, ". . . that I may make it manifest." Paul wanted to make it obvious to everyone that Christ's death on the cross was the only basis for a right standing with God. But to do so, he needed an opportunity.

Just as God has to bring an understanding of the Gospel to non-believers, He also has to provide us with the opportunity to present it. Since He is more desirous of the lost coming to Christ than we are, we can pray with confidence that as we ask, He *will* grant opportunities to share Christ with others.

Sometimes that opportunity comes much sooner than we think!

To illustrate

When our son, David, was quite young, he'd begin a conversation about Christ with a simple question, "What are you depending on to get you to heaven?" It's amazing how quickly that question opened up a discussion about spiritual things!

While visiting a neighbor, David whispered to his mom, "Is she a Christian?" Tammy whispered back, "Daddy and I don't know. We've been asking God to give us the opportunity to find out."

David decided this was his day of opportunity. So he approached her and asked, "What are you depending on to get you to heaven?" She answered, "Jesus Christ." He then asked, "Christ plus works or Christ alone?" At this she turned to Tammy and asked, "Would you please explain what it means to be born again?" and Tammy led her to Christ. A prayer for opportunity was answered.

To meditate

The God who works in astounding ways to bring the lost to Christ can, through prayer, provide the open door to bring Christ to the lost.

To pray

Think of three people you would like to see come to Christ. Ask God to give you an opportunity to speak to each one. Then be prepared to take advantage of the open doors.

8

Get Ready! Get Set!

To read

*Now it happened in Iconium that they went to-
gether to the synagogue of the Jews, and so spoke
that a great multitude both of the Jews and of
the Greeks believed* (Acts 14:1).

To consider

God sends powerful messages through His
Word. Sometimes we don't have to read a whole
chapter or a paragraph to learn something valu-
able or transforming. We often need to read only
one verse.

This is one of those verses. It has something very
important to say about evangelism that should impact our lives. The comment has been made that in
order to avoid criticism, say nothing, do nothing,
and be nothing. In Acts 13, Paul and Barnabas experienced blessing and conflict in Antioch as messengers of the Gospel. Multitudes are responding
to their message, but the religious leaders were not
happy. Stirring up the leaders and prominent people
of the city resulted in not only being pointed to the
exit, but escorted out of the city. As Paul and

Barnabas shook off the dust of the city just outside the city limits, they headed for Iconium.

When they got there, did they know what they were going to say and how they were going to say it? Very definitely. The text says they "so spoke that a great multitude both of the Jews and of the Greeks believed." That means they presented the Gospel in such a way that the hearer understood the message and their own need and responded to the invitation to believe in Christ. The point, simply put, is that Paul and Barnabas most definitely knew how to present the Gospel.

Those who know how to present the Gospel are characterized by effectiveness and consistency in evangelism. In fact, those consistent in presenting the Gospel have a basic method they use. They know how to go about speaking to lost people. If we desire to evangelize, we must learn how.

To illustrate

The Milwaukee Sentinel once quoted the story of a police officer who decided to take up deer hunting. The problem was he didn't know how to hunt deer. So one morning he went out in the middle of the woods and hid behind a bush. Much to his delight, a whitetail deer came trotting along. As the deer stepped in front of the bush, the man jumped out from the bush, fired a warning shot in the air, pointed his pistol at the deer, and shouted, "Freeze! Police!" If we are going to fish for the lost, we need to learn how.

To meditate

If someone only had five minutes to live and wanted to know how to get to heaven, what would you say? Could you explain it so simply that a child would understand?

To pray

Ask God to help you learn a method that will help you present the Gospel clearly. Interact with your church leaders about suggestions they may have, and be prepared to see Him answer your prayers.

9

It's Just Plain Scary!

To read

I was with you in weakness, in fear, and in much trembling (1 Corinthians 2:3).

To consider

I have never met anyone that isn't afraid of something. Surveys reveal that two of the most common fears are the fear of flying and the fear of speaking in public.

That second fear hits us in the area of publicly speaking the name of Christ—even if the audience is no more than one person. We probably think of Paul as a person who never knew such a fear. We imagine him as a bull in a china shop when it came to his personal witness. Evidence from Scripture would reveal the opposite to be true.

Look at the times he requested prayer for boldness (Eph. 6:19). And look at a text like the one above from 1 Corinthians. Weakness, fear, and trembling are three rather descriptive words to sum up Paul's demeanor in the city of Corinth. "Weakness" most likely refers to everything from the thorn in his flesh, whatever that could have been, to his unimpressive physical stature. "Fear" would likely be the result of the wickedness of the city that made him unpopular to the hostility of the Jews that made him unwanted. "Trembling" would most likely bring to mind the quivering of his body on the outside that reflected the nervousness on the inside.

Not exactly a macho-man appearance, is it? But don't overlook these four words: "I was with you." To Paul, the issue was never that he was afraid; that was a foregone conclusion. The issue was whether or not he would go ahead despite his fears. He seemed to be keenly aware that if he would deal with the matter of his obedience, God would deal with the matter of his fear by supplying the needed boldness.

To illustrate

A boy was given a part in a Christmas play. All he needed to do was walk out on stage, look at the audience, and say, "It's me. Be not afraid." When it came time to perform, he walked out on stage and, frozen with fright, said, "It's me, and I'm scared!" What an example of the feelings we suffer in evangelism! But nevertheless, he was there. Even when we're scared, we need to go ahead and speak to others, admitting to God we are afraid and asking Him to help us be obedient.

To meditate

God will always deal with the matter of your fear if you will simply deal with the matter of your obedience.

To pray

Don't say to God, "Help me not to be afraid to talk about you." Recognize that fear is normal. Instead pray, "Help me to go ahead, just like Paul did, in spite of my fears." Then prepare yourself for the next fearful opportunity when He can answer those prayers and make you bold.

10

With Whom Are You Trying to Impress Them?

To read

> *And I, brethren, when I came to you, did not come with excellence of speech or of wisdom declaring to you the testimony of God. For I determined not to know anything among you except Jesus Christ and Him crucified* (1 Corinthians 2:1–2).

To consider

Pride and the desire to impress people can enter into anything we do—even evangelism. Should a non-Christian become argumentative, we can seek to prove that our mind is faster and our tongue sharper. Only one person usually wins such a discussion—Satan.

Paul's words are shocking. Corinth was filled with intellectuals and philosophers—people who loved to impress others with their oratorical skills. You would think Paul would have tried to outwit them. With his knowledge of the Greek language and Roman customs, there is no doubt he could have won any debate into which he was cast. Instead, he made it clear that his message was not character-ized by fancy words or philosophical depth. Instead, Paul focused all his brilliance and intellect on simply presenting the Person and work of Christ on the cross. He never felt the need to be a philosopher or debater. He was a proclaimer.

What a freeing thought in evangelism! God is not expecting us to be able to refute every objection non-Christians give or answer any question they raise. We are to simply lay before them the Person and work of Christ. We want to impress them with Him, not our own intellect or ability.

To illustrate

Dawson Trotman, founder of the Navigators, once said, "Soulwinners are not soulwinners because of what they know, but because of Who they know and how much they want others to know Him."

To meditate

Upon hearing Paul present his message, a non-Christian would not have been likely to say, "What a brilliant speaker," but instead, "What a beautiful Savior!"

To pray

Evangelism is only effective as we keep ourselves out of the picture and make the Savior the focus of attention. Have you found yourself falling into a trap that makes you think that to reach the lost you must outwit them? Ask God to help you focus the lost on Christ. Ask Him to help you be first and foremost a proclaimer.

11

Lord, Increase the Tribe

To read

After these things the Lord appointed seventy others also, and sent them two by two before His face into every city and place where He Himself was about to go. Then He said to them, "The harvest truly is great, but the laborers are few; therefore pray the Lord of the harvest to send out laborers into His harvest" (Luke 10:1–2).

To consider

Have you ever thought how many times you've uttered the words, "There's not enough"? We may be referring to the limited supply of ice we've bought along for the community picnic or the insufficient number of people present to move a piano into the next room. Whether at home or at work, in the midst of our business or in the middle of our play, we may have reason to exclaim, "There's not enough!"

There is never enough in evangelism. Evangelism is not something that believers gravitate to, though they should. Any function on a church calendar will receive greater response than a plea to get involved in evangelism. There may not be enough workers to canvas a community for an evangelism rally, enough help to sponsor and promote a friendship dinner for non-Christians, or enough workers to help with vacation Bible school.

Prayer is not *an* answer—it's *the* answer. God has to raise up workers. As Christ prepared to send out the seventy, two by two, His concern was that there be a lot more than just those. Faced with the enormous potential of the harvest, He said, "Pray for laborers."

All of our pleading and begging for people to get involved in evangelism will have little effect if it's not bathed in prayer. When specific prayer for laborers is offered, individuals came forth with a very simple testimony, "For some reason, God has burdened me to get more involved in evangelism."

To illustrate

A professional football player was once asked, "What is the greatest contribution football has made to physical fitness?"

He answered, "None."

Surprised, they asked, "None?"

He responded, "Football is often twenty-two people on the field desperately needing rest and fifty-two thousand in the stands desperately needing exercise."

How often those statistics are true in evangelism. We must pray for more laborers.

To meditate

Those experienced in evangelism have discovered that there are often more unbelievers willing to listen than there are believers willing to talk.

To pray

What evangelistic outreach is your church contemplating? Have *you* offered to assist? As you do, ask God to burden other people within your church whom He would have participate. As you see individuals responding, ask God to make you an encouragement to them.

12

When All Else Fails, Just Follow

To read

> *Now Jesus, walking by the Sea of Galilee, saw two brothers, Simon called Peter, and Andrew his brother, casting a net into the sea; for they were fishermen. And He said to them, "Follow Me, and I will make you fishers of men"* (Matthew 4:18–19).

To consider

Ever think what a hopeless group of men (humanly speaking, that is) Christ started out with to transform the world? They didn't know the slightest thing about evangelism. After all, they put bread on the table with their fishing skills, not their people skills.

In addition, look at a few specific personalities. Take Peter, for example. On the one hand, he could be so courageous that he'd attempt to walk on water. On the other hand, he could be so cowardly that he'd deny knowing his Master. He was self-giving one day and self-serving the next.

Peter had no formal education, no ministry experience, and quite a few character flaws. How could God use *him?* Very simply. Jesus didn't say, "Follow me because you are fishers of men."

Instead, His exact words were, "Follow me, and I will *make* you fishers of men." The disciples understood one thing. All they had to do was follow, and He would teach them all they needed to know.

That's all God wants us to do—just follow, and as we do, He'll develop us and teach us everything we need to know to evangelize. When all else fails, just follow!

To illustrate

A grandfather used to go on long walks and talks with his grandson. As he was preparing to leave one day, he asked his grandson, "Do you want to go with me?" The grandson asked, "Where are you going?" The grandfather took off without him. When he returned, the grandson asked, "Why didn't you take me with you?" The grandfather explained, "Because you asked me where I was going. If you really wanted to go with me, it would not have mattered where I was going." When it comes to evangelism, just follow. He'll do the rest.

To meditate

If you want to know how to talk to nonbelievers, just walk with the Master Fisherman. He'll show you.

To pray

Have you often felt that you just don't know enough to be good in evangelism? Evangelism is first and foremost an issue of discipleship. Ask God to help you follow Him one day at a time in each area of your life. Then ask Him to help you learn what He wants to teach you about touching people for eternity.

13

Die Later—but Decide Now!

To read

> Then all the tax collectors and the sinners drew
> near to Him to hear Him. And the Pharisees and
> scribes murmured, saying, "This man receives
> sinners and eats with them" (Luke 15:1–2).

To consider

Years ago my good friend and mentor Dr. Haddon
Robinson made a thought-provoking statement to
our fourth-year class at seminary. He said, "You
ought to decide now what you want people to carve
on your tombstone. Then live your life backwards
from there."

That thought hit me like a boulder. Each time
I've thought of it, I've said to myself, What greater
thing could be written on anyone's tombstone than
that label ascribed to Christ: "friend of sinners." It
seems like Christ always had a reputation for being
with the wrong people at the wrong time in the
wrong place. But He deserved that reputation. After
all, He worked hard to earn it!

So great was His reputation in that area that if
He were to walk the streets today, do you realize

who would be most likely to walk up and greet Him? Predominantly, they would not be the higher-ups of society; they'd be the down-and-outers, the people who needed Him and *knew* they needed Him.

How Christlike are we? Research shows that two years after a person is converted, they've dropped most of their non-Christian friends. For sure, fellowship with Christians is essential. But so is contact with the lost. A good barometer of your spiritual temperature is how many good friendships you have with non-Christians with a vision of leading them to Christ.

To illustrate

A Christian veterinarian once described his occupation to a Christian brother. He explained, "The veterinary practice is how I put food on my table. But my occupation is introducing people to Jesus Christ. The veterinary practice just gives me the opportunity to get to know them and spend time with them." Regardless of our profession, that ought to be our testimony.

To meditate

If someone were to write a phrase on your tombstone that captured your life, what would it be?

To pray

Think of a few non-Christians you don't know very well. Ask God to develop your relationship with those people. Think of things you might do with them, and ask God for wisdom and direction in being a better friend to them. Build a relationship that might be a bridge to the Gospel.

14

I Don't Enjoy Non-Christians

To read

> *But when He saw the multitudes, He was moved with compassion for them, because they were weary and scattered, like sheep having no shepherd* (Matthew 9:36).

To consider

"I don't enjoy being around non-Christians." If I've heard that statement once, I've heard it at least fifty times. I always respond, "Who does? They can be selfish, inconsiderate, rude, and obnoxious," and then I add, "just like some believers!"

The Bible never asks, "Do you enjoy non-Christians?" Instead it would ask, "Do you pity them?" That's what the word "compassion" means—to be filled with pity. Eight times in the New Testament it says that Christ was filled with pity toward the lost. The verse above explains why—they were like sheep having no shepherd. In other words, He looked beyond the person to the problem, beyond the conduct at the condition.

Unbelievers act the way they do because they are the people they are—controlled by Satan, dead in trespasses and sins, without the controlling power of the Holy Spirit. They have no choice but to act, talk, and believe as Satan directs.

When we contemplate that reality, our hearts go out in pity toward non-Christians. No longer do we concern ourselves with whether or not we enjoy them. The issue is whether or not we *pity* them. That in itself moves our hearts in their direction and causes us to reach out to them with the message of the saving grace of Christ.

To illustrate

In the 1950s Christians were shocked and saddened to hear of the tragic deaths of five young missionaries who were killed by the Auca Indians of Ecuador. They had believed the Indians to be friendly and had landed on a stretch of sandy beach hoping to begin friendly communication with the natives. It was there they met their death, martyrs for the cause of Christ. The father of one of the martyred men made a most interesting statement when he said, "I feel more sorry for these poor Indians than for my own son." Compassion makes a difference.

To meditate

God never asks, "Do you enjoy non-Christians?" He simply asks, "Do you pity them?"

To pray

Take five minutes and consider what the most annoying things about you were before you came to Christ. Then do two things: (1) Praise God for the individual or individuals who looked beyond those faults and led you to the Savior, and (2) ask God to help you begin to see lost people the way He sees them—as sheep without a shepherd.

15

The Proper
Fear in Evangelism

To read

> *Whatever I tell you in the dark, speak in the light;
> and what you hear in the ear, preach on the
> housetops. And do not fear those who kill the
> body but cannot kill the soul. But rather fear Him
> who is able to destroy both soul and body in hell*
> (Matthew 10:27–28).

To consider

The comment has been made that the cross was
not the Favorite Citizen Award given to Jesus by
the Jerusalem Chamber of Commerce. Instead, it
represented all the hostility His message received
and the fact that as far as the rulers were concerned,
He deserved the death of a criminal.

Jesus Christ made it clear to His disciples that they
would not win popularity contests. Nevertheless, He
encouraged them to be bold in the proclamation of
His truth. What He told them in private, they were to
repeat in public. What He whispered in their ears,
they were to shout from the housetops.

What did He expect the disciples' reaction to be? Fear. Not the fear of dangerous villains and angry mobs—but fear of God who controls their eternal destiny. God didn't mean that we should be frightened of him. Instead, the fear of God means we so revere and respect Him that the mere thought of doing contrary to what He desires is something we abhor. We should take our instructions from Christ. To disappoint Him means everything. To disappoint people means nothing.

As we seek to be His disciples in evangelism, the fear of God ought to control us. We must so reverence Him for His awesomeness that we serve Him with an attitude that says, Nothing more, nothing less, nothing else. Knowing His heart for lost people, we are compelled to reach out to the same people to whom He reached out.

To illustrate

Carved on the tombstone of a man noted for his evangelistic zeal were the simple words, "He feared men so little because He feared God so much."

To meditate

In evangelism, the fear of God is the greatest remedy there is for the fear of people.

To pray

Think about ten things that demonstrate the awesomeness of God, such as His beauty in the universe, the birth of a child, and your own salvation. Ask God to give you a keen awareness of who He is as you have opportunity to evangelize—an awareness that makes the responses and reactions of others less intimidating to you.

16

Kind to Whom?
You Must Be Kidding!

To read

> *For we ourselves were also once foolish, disobedient, deceived, serving various lusts and pleasures, living in malice and envy, hateful and hating one another. But when the kindness and the love of God our Savior toward man appeared, not by works of righteousness which we have done, but according to His mercy He saved us, through the washing of regeneration and renewing of the Holy Spirit* (Titus 3:3–5).

To consider

The Scriptures speak of our need to be kind toward others. Simply put, the word *kindness* means to have a good, generous, and giving spirit. Everything about us was distasteful to God. But God had a good, generous, and giving spirit. He allowed His Son to die on a cross in our place and take the punishment that we deserved so that through personal trust in Him we could receive the gift of eternal life.

With that in mind, we ought to ask ourselves, "Who am I kind toward?" We probably think of our best friends for whom we've done favors. As needful as that is, those are not the ones the Scriptures flag as the people Christ was kind towards. We are told, "He is kind to the unthankful and evil" (Luke 6:35). Our kindness ought to be seen in the way we respond to a non-Christian for whom we've done so much but received so little. It ought to be seen toward the fellow employee who has never met the Savior and, for that reason, often misrepresents us to others. Just as He was kind to us in our lost condition, we, in turn, ought to be kind to others.

To illustrate

A man on a business trip was mistreated by a member of his business concern. As he was relating the incident to a friend, the friend asked, "What did you do to that man? A man like that ought to be taught a lesson." The businessman responded, "Oh, I didn't do a thing. I'm not here to avenge personal wrongs. I'm on business for my employer."

As a believer, do you see yourself on earth to avenge personal wrongs or on business for your employer—Jesus Christ? If you're on business for your employer, that will entail the need to be kind toward those who may be unkind. Your kindness could lead to an opportunity to present the Savior.

To meditate

The dynamic of discipleship is not being kind toward the people who are kind toward you. Instead, it is being kind toward those who are the opposite toward you.

To pray

Think of a non-Christian you know, perhaps one who has not treated you appropriately or who has hurt you in one way or another. Then ask yourself, In what way can I extend kindness to that person? Pray and ask God to use whatever you decide upon as an expression of the love of Christ to give you an opportunity to share the gift of Christ—eternal life.

17

Is Your Life an Illustration?

To read

> *Bearing with one another, and forgiving one another, if anyone has a complaint against another; even as Christ forgave you, so you also must do* (Colossians 3:13).

To consider

There are times that individuals very near and dear to me play practical jokes on me. At times, they get brutal and give me extensive teasing—all undeserved, of course! At those times, I love to look at them and exclaim, "Now you know why I minister to unbelievers. I can't stand Christians!"

I'm only joking, of course. But more times than I like to admit, I've had to reflect upon the sad truth of that statement. There are Christians I've known who are some of the most deceptive, hateful, and backbiting people one could meet. Needless to say, they're usually not impacting anyone for Christ. If anything, they are turning non-Christians away from Him.

What bothers me the most is when I observe an unforgiving spirit, because forgiveness is one of the things most noted about Christ and should be most noted about us. But this text does not say, "Forgive because Christ forgave you," but *"even as"* Christ forgave you." That means totally and completely— never to mention the wrong again. How are others going to understand the depth of His forgiveness if they have not experienced the depth of ours? No wonder God says, "So also you must do." What a powerful way to illustrate His forgiveness—let them see ours.

To illustrate

During a war in Turkey, a soldier pursued a girl and her brother, brutally murdering the boy. The girl escaped. She later got a job as a nurse in a hospital in that area. One day, they brought in a soldier whom she recognized as the one who had murdered her brother. One slip of her hand would have meant his death. But she, being a Christian, took care of him and nursed him back to health.

When he recovered, he, too, recognized her and asked the obvious question, "Why didn't you try to get revenge for the slaying of your brother?"

She answered, "Because I'm a Christian. The Bible says love your enemies and do good to those who hate you." He responded, "I never knew there was such a religion. Tell me about it. I want it."

To meditate

If a non-Christian has not experienced your forgiveness, how can you expect that person to be attracted to His?

To pray

Is there *anyone* in your life to whom you've not extended the forgiveness God has given you? If so, call that what God calls it: sin. Tell God that you are extending to that person the forgiveness He has extended to you. Then, acting on your prayer, do whatever you need to do to restore the relationship.

18

Teamwork

To read

For in this the saying is true: "One sows and an-other reaps." I sent you to reap that for which you have not labored; others have labored, and you have entered into their labors (John 4:37–38).

To consider

We are not living in a result-oriented society. We are living in an *instant* result-oriented society. In the morning, we can help ourselves to instant coffee. Should we need to drop clothes off at the dry clean-ers, they will promise to have them ready in one hour. Should the car need an oil change, we can take ad-vantage of an instant oil change. Should we drop by a restaurant for lunch, many places advertise that if your lunch isn't at your table in ten minutes, it's free.

That's one reason we suffer when it comes to evangelism. Every person we share Christ with we want to come to Christ—*now!* If our motive were the brevity of life and the fear that they could die without Christ, it wouldn't be so bad. The truth is, however, that we simply don't want to do the long-term sowing of seed and cultivating of a stubborn soul.

We must understand in a fresh way that there are those with whom faithfulness means we will be the sixth of six people to help bring this person to Christ. But faithfulness with others means we must be willing to be the seventh of eighteen, the ninth of twelve, or the second of twenty-two. Either way, both the sower and the reaper have their reward. It's a team of people, often unknown to each other, that God uses to bring a person to Christ.

To illustrate

While sitting on a plane, I once engaged in conversation with the teenager next to me. He told me his aunt and uncle were shipping him off to Texas to live with another aunt and uncle. My heart went out to him. When he asked, "What do you do?" I answered, "I'm a minister."

He then proceeded to explain that a group of high school students at his school met for prayer each morning and had been speaking to him about Jesus Christ. When I asked if any of them had ever taken a Bible and shown him how he could know he was going to heaven, he said, "No." When I asked if I could, he responded, "Would you?"

There at 30,000 feet above sea level, I had the privilege of leading him to Christ. When I stepped off the plane, I was grateful to God for the privilege of reaping, but just as grateful for those high school students who were faithful in sowing. We all need each other.

To meditate

God might use you to bring someone to Christ. Other times He might use you to simply bring them one step closer to the kingdom.

To pray

Do you feel like a failure if the person you speak to does not come to Christ? Ask God to help you to be willing to do the reaping for some and the sowing for others. Ask Him to make you a team player.

19

Having a Problem with Patience?

To read

But we were gentle among you, just as a nursing mother cherishes her own children (1 Thessalonians 2:7).

To consider

Most of us will admit that patience is not one of our virtues. More times than we'd like to admit, we are like the person who prayed, "God give me patience, and give it to me now!"

Sometimes our impatience is most evident when it comes to those who have just entered the family of God. We often want new believers to be in five days at a point it took us five years to achieve. Should they *immediately* not hunger for the Word, spend time in prayer, desire fellowship with believers, clean up their language, and renounce their bad habits, we can become terribly impatient with them. Our impatience is sometimes seen in the way we become judgmental towards them, critical of their actions, and sometimes untrusting of their sincerity.

In one word, what is needed is gentleness—the gentleness that Paul the apostle compares to a nursing mother cherishing her own children. Have you ever thought of the fits we may have put our nursing mother through— infant illnesses for which time and patience were the only cures, self-centered behavior, unreasonable demands, midnight feedings, perpetual care, and dirty diapers?

That kind of care and concern, patience and perseverance, time and toil is what it often takes to see new Christians grow. That's especially true in the '90s when those coming to Christ are beset with more past sins and problems and fewer moral standards than ever before.

To illustrate

A lifeguard was once asked how he would teach a girl to swim. He took thirty minutes to explain in painstaking detail how he would do it in a way that applauded his patience.

He was then asked, "But suppose that girl was your little sister." He remarked, "Oh, in that case, I'd just take her to the edge and push her in."

Once non-Christians come to Christ by faith, we cannot show them how to swim the Christian life by standing on the edge and saying, "Lots of luck!" We must jump in with them and help them through those initial struggles and temptations.

To meditate

It may take fifteen minutes of your time to lead a person to Christ but five years of your time to help them grow. How much are you willing to give?

To pray

Think of a new Christian you know. Ask God to show you something tangible you can do this week to encourage that individual in his or her spiritual growth.

20

Too Good to
Keep to Ourselves

To read

> *But to him who does not work but believes on Him who justifies the ungodly, his faith is accounted for righteousness* (Romans 4:5).

To consider

Have you ever noticed how much we grade people on the basis of their performance? Our whole society has gotten in on the action. School teachers do it, parents do it, employers do it, even wardens in prisons do it. The better we perform, the higher up the ladder we go; the more we make, the greater privileges we receive or the fewer penalties we suffer.

I am convinced that this emphasis on performance is one reason non-Christians may find it hard to grasp the grace of God and His *free* gift of life eternal. They are trying to understand God's love by *comparing* rather than *contrasting* it to human love. As one non-Christian whom I had the privilege of leading to Christ said, "I always thought the harder you worked, the higher you went."

No verse of Scripture could make it any clearer that a right standing before God has nothing to do with our worth, merit, or work than Romas 4:5. Imperfect people that we are, we cannot pay for our own sins. Only the perfect Son of God could do that. Since He has died on a cross for our sins and risen victoriously, we simply need to believe—trust in Christ alone to save us. God will justify or declare us righteous, not based on what we've done for God, but based on what Christ did for us.

The reason is that "his faith is accounted for righteousness." That simply means that when we trust Christ, God takes the perfection of His Son and places it over us. Therefore, when He looks on us, He no longer sees our sin; He only sees the perfection of His Son. We are forever accepted by God, not based on our performance but based on His.

That is too good and too great a gift to keep to ourselves. The awesome recognition of the depth of the grace of God ought to move us to tell somebody else. After all, we have first-hand knowledge of something unbelievers won't find or experience anywhere else.

To illustrate

A professional athlete broke an eighteen-year-old record in his field because of his tremendous agility and coordination. As he envisioned his name in the *Guinness Book of World Records*, he anticipated the many invitations to appear on talk shows across America. His concern at the moment, though, was using his talent to help develop the athletic ability of young people. As he acknowledged that his gift came from God, he explained, "Anytime you have a special gift like this, you have to share it with others."

How much more true is that statement for those who have received the free spiritual gift of eternal life through Christ's substitutionary death and resurrection.

To meditate

If evangelism is one beggar telling another beggar where to find bread, why not direct non-Christians to the buffet?

To pray

Once we come to Christ, how quickly we forget the depth and the freeness of our salvation. Ask God to remind you of the supremacy of the grace that brought you to the Savior. Out of gratitude for His love, tell someone about Him.

21

The Right Kind of Preoccupation

To read

Therefore do not worry, saying, "What shall we eat?" or "What shall we drink?" or "What shall we wear?" For after all these things the Gentiles seek. For your heavenly Father knows that you need all these things. But seek first the kingdom of God and His righteousness, and all these things shall be added to you (Matthew 6:31–33).

To consider

Anxiety has a way of plaguing our lives—worries about the children, our health, our job, our finances, and our future. Some medical doctors have even estimated that over twenty-five percent of their patient load is what they call "the worry well." Doctors spend a considerable chunk of their time examining people who are not sick; they're only worried.

For a Christian, there is a tremendous source of comfort when faced with worry. We can take anything that is on our shoulders and, through prayer, push it onto His—knowing His shoulders are so much bigger than ours. We are told in Scripture that upon doing so, "The peace of God, which surpasses all understanding, will guard your hearts and minds through Christ Jesus" (Phil. 4:7).

But this paragraph also has an interesting remedy to worry. Christ speaks in terms of physical needs—food, water, and clothing—and then says, "Seek first the kingdom of God and His righteousness and all these things shall be added to you."

His advice is simple and direct. If we concern ourselves with His business, He concerns Himself with ours. In essence, He is saying, "If you are going to worry, worry about having a consistent prayer life, or spending time in the Word, or introducing a neighbor to Christ. And if you concern yourself with My business, I'll concern Myself with yours." Be preoccupied with the right thing.

To illustrate

Queen Elizabeth I once asked a servant of hers if he'd go on a matter of foreign business for her. Although he expressed a desire to please her, he also expressed concern about matters at home that would be left unattended.

She promptly replied, "You take care of my business, I'll take care of yours."

God does not expect us to neglect our family, job, or financial matters. He also does not want unnecessary anxiety in those areas to prevent us from taking the time to introduce lost acquaintances to Christ.

To meditate

When it comes to anxiety, are you following the example of others or setting the example for others to follow? Can others see His concerns by observing yours?

To pray

Ask God to give you a proper concern about physical matters that relate to your home, family, and job. But ask Him to keep you from an anxious concern about day-to-day necessities that keep you from having the time and interest to be used by Him in populating heaven.

22

Dare to Be Different!

To read

Do all things without murmuring and disputing, that you may become blameless and harmless, children of God without fault in the midst of a crooked and perverse generation, among whom you shine as lights in the world, holding fast the word of life, so that I may rejoice in the day of Christ that I have not run in vain or labored in vain (Philippians 2:14–16).

To consider

Imagine that a believer were to ask you, "How can I live, talk, and act in such a way that would bring people to Christ?" How would you respond? Many of us would give a five hundred-word answer because we have ways of beating around the bush and making things complicated.

Paul the apostle, though, cuts right to the chase. He speaks of the need for believers to be blameless and harmless as they hold forth the Word of Life. His exhortation is, "Do all things without murmuring and disputing." Paul is referring to a person who enjoys spending time in front of the complaint counter. Do you know someone who always finds something wrong with people and situations?

Paul also refers to a person who always questions what God says and sits in judgment of it. When God says to forgive others, the disputer may refuse because "they wouldn't appreciate it." In essence, they argue with everyone, including God.

Paul says to do everything without complaining or arguing. Why? Your attitude will be so different than that of the crooked and perverse generation you live in. Before you know it, conversations might open up to share the Gospel.

To illustrate

An issue of *Reader's Digest* carried the story of a car at a crowded intersection that stalled, holding up traffic. Obviously frustrated, the woman driver got out and lifted the hood to see if she could determine the problem. Almost immediately, the driver behind her, also frustrated, began honking his horn.

Soon, being frustrated with both her car and him, the woman walked back to him and said, "I'll make you a deal. If you go up there and fix my car, I'll sit here and honk your horn for you."

"Honkers" don't attract people to Christ. They are too much like the world they are trying to reach.

To meditate

Don't practice the three C's of the world— complaining, criticizing, and condemning. Practice God's three E's—evangelizing, equipping, and encouraging.

To pray

If you have allowed negative thinking and a chronic complaining attitude to creep into your life, ask God to forgive you and remove it so that your witness for the Savior is not impaired.

23

Basic Football

To read

I charge you therefore before God and the Lord Jesus Christ, who will judge the living and the dead at His appearing and His kingdom: Preach the word! Be ready in season and out of season. Convince, rebuke, exhort, with all longsuffering and teaching. For the time will come when they will not endure sound doctrine, but according to their own desires, because they have itching ears, they will heap up for themselves teachers; and they will turn their ears away from the truth, and be turned aside to fables. But you be watchful in all things, endure afflictions, do the work of an evangelist, fulfill your ministry (2 Timothy 4:1–5).

To consider

In light of Christ's return, the apostle Paul gives advice to Timothy concerning the responsibility God placed on him as a pastor and teacher. He clearly states the what, the how, and the why. Timothy is to preach the Word. It is to be done in season, out of season, and with all longsuffering. The time is coming when people will no longer want sound teaching.

But with the need for the truth, the pastor or teacher dare not forget their need to reach out. Paul exhorts Timothy to do the work of an evangelist.

Many pastors have confessed this to be the weak part of their ministry. Stressed for time, evangelism takes the hardest hit. Then, too, they suffer the same struggles we all do in evangelism—fear. What pastors need most are your prayers that God will help them to be examples and not just exhorters in evangelism. The "basic football" of ministry is teaching the believer *and* reaching the lost.

To illustrate

Reader's Digest told of a man delivering an old typewriter to a city mission. Unable to open the door, he noticed a sign: Door sticks—Pull hard! After trying endlessly, he placed his foot against the door and ended up with the doorknob in his hand. He then noticed the second sign: Closed Wednesdays. God has not given pastors one instruction, but two: Teach the believers *and* reach the lost. Unless both are obeyed, the Great Commission has not been fulfilled.

To meditate

The reason that many have not been drawn to the Savior's doctrine is that they have not been introduced to the Savior's death.

To pray

Think of two pastors you know. Ask God to help them find the needed time to be examples to others in evangelism. As you do, ask God to help you be part of the solution, not the problem, in terms of the demands you make on them.

24

Good-bye, Guilt Trip

To read

Moreover it is required in stewards that one be found faithful (1 Corinthians 4:2).

To consider

Many believers feel that all evangelism is is a guilt trip, and when they do share Christ, it's because they feel like they have to, not because they want to. Evangelism isn't exciting. It's a headache.

Why? There are undoubtedly several reasons, but one would definitely be the prevailing notion that God holds us responsible for fruit. That is, if we share the Savior with the lost and they don't trust Him, God is disappointed in us.

Wait a minute! First Corinthians 4:2 doesn't say, "Moreover it is required in stewards that one be found fruitful." Instead, it says it is required that one be found *faithful*. That was Paul's own testimony as the Corinthians were quick to judge both his actions and his motives. In evangelism, that takes the burden from my shoulders and puts it on His. I just have to be faithful in bringing *Christ* to *them*. It's God's responsibility to bring *them* to *Christ*.

What a freeing thought in evangelism! I can enjoy the experience, become one person wiser every time I do it, and recognize that the results are in God's hands. If I share the Gospel and the person doesn't see his need, I have been just as faithful as if he had trusted Christ. God tells me to be faithful, not fruitful.

To illustrate

A man from California was visiting his sister in Tulsa, Oklahoma, whom he had not seen for over twenty years. She had told him, "If you come to see me, I ask that you come with me to my church on Sunday and hear a guest speaker who's an evangelist."

He came to church and, the next day, came to Christ. He then testified, "I can't wait to get back to California. A church there has been praying for over twenty years that I'd come to Christ."

If we concern ourselves with being faithful, God will concern Himself with seeing that, in His time, we are fruitful.

To meditate

If you take the responsibility to be faithful, God will take the responsibility to bear fruit.

To pray

Ask God to help you keep the right focus in evangelism. Ask Him to remind you with each opportunity you have in evangelism that God simply wants you to bring Christ to the lost, recognizing that only He can bring the lost to Christ.

25

Living Life Backwards?

To read

For what is our hope, or joy, or crown of rejoic-
ing? Is it not even you in the presence of our
Lord Jesus Christ at His coming? For you are
our glory and joy (1 Thessalonians 2:19–20).

To consider

Priorities. Such a frustrating word, isn't it? Yet
it's the one that will determine whether or not we
have lived a worthwhile life. What sadder
experience could there be than to come to the end
and discover that we have lived for things that are
going up in smoke. And what more exciting
experience could there be than to realize we have
been faithful and lived for the things that really
count.

What is one way to keep these priorities in check?
Imagine that you have just died and are standing
face-to-face with Jesus. What will you wish had
been the most important items in your life? Will
they be the TV and the VCR, the new house or
expensive car, the golf course or the swimming
pool? Or will it be what it was for Paul the apostle—

the ones he had led to Christ and the ones God allowed him to disciple?

As Paul said to the Thessalonians, "For what is our hope, or joy, or crown of rejoicing? Is it not even *you*?" Paul had been instrumental in leading many of them to Christ and then caring for them as a nursing mother does her own children to help them grow (1 Thess. 2:7). Because he lived for people, not things, the day he anticipated seeing Christ face-to-face was to be his most exciting one ever.

Live life from heaven backwards. Whatever is going to be important then, make it important now. When you stand before Christ, there will be no remorse or regrets. That thought alone ought to motivate us to introduce a lost person to Christ.

To illustrate

A man known in history as the Earl of Rochester lived a wealthy but wicked life. When he came to the end of his life, he exclaimed, "Would to God I had been born a blind beggar or a foul leper rather than to have lived and forgotten God."

What appeared to distress him as his life came to an end is that he had lived for all the things that really didn't matter. If we are not careful, even though we are believers who worship the name of Christ, we can live for all the things that, when we are face-to-face with Christ, won't matter, instead of for the people who will.

To meditate

Think carefully. Is there someone in whose life you were a messenger of His saving grace? Do you have someone who is your "crown of rejoicing"?

To pray

Make a list of what should be most important in your life as you anticipate seeing Christ face-to-face. Then take that list and, in prayer, ask God to help you master your priorities until you come to a point that God's priorities have mastered you.

26

Beyond Your Greatest Imagination

To read

> *In My Father's house are many mansions; if it were not so, I would have told you. I go to prepare a place for you. And if I go and prepare a place for you, I will come again and receive you to Myself; that where I am, there you may be also* (John 14:2–3).

To consider

Have you ever tried to imagine what heaven is going to be like? While I was in college, a few of us stayed up to a ridiculous hour trying to figure out and imagine the beauties of the place. We found verses in the book of Revelation helpful and absolutely exciting, but we still didn't have all the details. Simply put, the information we have about heaven in the Scriptures is rather limited.

Ever wonder why? I would not pretend to have all the answers, but I think I have a good hunch. If God were ever to try and tell us what the mansion is like that He is preparing for us, we, with our limited, finite minds would not even be able to comprehend it.

Take a moment and think about the most beautiful picture you have ever seen, the most magnificent landscape you've ever set your eyes on, or the most gorgeous scene that's ever been described to you. I am convinced even those don't come *close* to the beauty of heaven. Concerning spiritual things and our inability to understand, God says, "Eye has not seen, nor ear heard, nor have entered into the heart of man the things which God has prepared for those who love him" (1 Cor. 2:9). In the realm of what He is designing for us in heaven, the same could safely be said.

What a motive to evangelize! With no more than a glimpse of its beauty, those going to heaven should not be content to go alone. Although I've never been able to locate the source, I have often recalled the words penned by another: "When I stand in that heavenly city and saints around me appear, I hope somebody comes up and says, 'You're the one who invited me here.'"

To illustrate

A girl was standing with her father admiring the evening sky. She said, "If it's that beautiful on this side, just think what the other side is going to look like."

To meditate

Other than the reward waiting for you when you arrive, the only thing you can take to heaven with you is a friend.

To pray

After reflecting upon His magnificent creation seen on earth, praise Him for what heaven is going to look like. Then talk to Him about a family member or friend you would like to have with you in His presence. Ask Him for an open door to present the Gospel to that person.

27

Wait Until You Hear This!

To read

For when we were still without strength, in due time Christ died for the ungodly. For scarcely for a righteous man will one die; yet perhaps for a good man someone would even dare to die. But God demonstrates His own love toward us, in that while we were still sinners, Christ died for us (Romans 5:6–8).

To consider

Have you ever compared your love to God's love? Compare the people for whom you would die to the people for whom He died.

A righteous person is someone who does what is proper. If you leave your house with the front door unlocked, whether for a day or a week, the righteous person will not enter it. Your house is not theirs. A good person not only does what is proper, but they do what is good. If you're in the hospital, the good person will pick up your paper and mow your lawn for you.

So here's the point—would you be willing to die for a righteous person? You respect him, but you wouldn't die for him. Perhaps for a really good person you might be willing to die. But God demonstrated His love in that He died for sinners. What you might do for the best, He did for the worst. What you might do for the deserving, He did for the undeserving.

Love like that can't be kept to ourselves. It has to be shared. What a privilege to introduce lost people to a love found only in Christ!

To illustrate

Years ago when steamers would go up and down the Mississippi, two of them passed each other. A foreman from down below on one of the steamers came up on deck and stood alongside a well-dressed gentleman.

Pointing to the other ship, he yelled, "There's the captain! There's the captain!"

The gentleman, a bit annoyed, said, "So what? Every ship has a captain."

The man answered, "That one's different. Once I was on his ship. A storm arose, and I was thrown overboard. I can't swim to save myself. He yanked off his cap, kicked off his shoes, threw off his coat, jumped overboard, and saved my life. Now, every time I have the opportunity, I just love to point him out."

What a privilege to point Him out!

To meditate

Anyone could have devised a way whereby people, if they were good, could get to heaven. It took a God of love to devise a way whereby all of us as sinners could make it.

To pray

The next time you have opportunity to share Christ, ask God to help you reflect on the question "How can I not share Christ?" instead of the question, "Must I?"

28

Beam It Out

To read

You are the light of the world. A city that is set on a hill cannot be hidden. Nor do they light a lamp and put it under a basket, but on a lampstand, and it gives light to all who are in the house. Let your light so shine before men, that they may see your good works and glorify your Father in heaven (Matthew 5:14–16).

To consider

Contractors would not build a city on a hill to hide it. They would build a city on a hill so everybody around can see it. In the same way, you don't take lamps and put them under bushels. The word *basket* here actually means a peck measure used for measuring corn. It was a common piece of furniture. You don't put a lamp under a basket. Instead, you put it on a lampstand—a stand specifically made for such a lamp so that in its elevated position, it would give light to the entire house.

Christ then makes His point. Don't hide your Christianity. Let your light so shine that others may see your good works and glorify your Father in heaven. Take your faith with you to college. Practice it on the job. Let it be seen in the department store. Carry it with you to school. Demonstrate it as a teacher. Demonstrate it as a parent. Practice it as a healthcare worker or hairdresser. Let people see your goodness and your good works. When Christians do good, they point people to a God who is even better.

You may be the only Christian on your job or in your neighborhood. But God has you there for a reason. He wants you to be the city on a hill and the light on a lampstand. Don't be discouraged, be encouraged. God can use you to accomplish something eternal.

To illustrate

One time, through an evangelistic outreach, a poor, destitute man came to Christ. As he later shared his testimony, a big, burly and boisterous non-Christian interrupted, "Wake up, old man. You're dreaming."

The poor man's little girl stepped up to the teaser and said, "Please, sir, don't wake him up. That's my daddy, and he is such a good daddy now. He used to beat my mother and spend all our money. We were all so miserable. But when he started 'dreaming,' everything changed. He is kind to all of us and provides for each of us. So if he's dreaming, please don't wake him up!"

To meditate

Words and actions are good when they point people to a Savior who is even better.

To pray

Have you thanked God lately for the many non-Christians around you and accepted your position as a strategic assignment from God? Ask God to use you as a consistent Christian whose light cannot be hidden.

29

Not Plus . . . Period!

To read

> *But now the righteousness of God apart from the law is revealed, being witnessed by the Law and the Prophets, even the righteousness of God which is through faith in Jesus Christ to all and on all who believe. For there is no difference; for all have sinned and fall short of the glory of God, being justified freely by His grace through the redemption that is in Christ Jesus* (Romans 3:21–24).

To consider

Why do those who grow up on the wrong side of the tracks often find coming to Christ easier than those who grow up on the right side?

One reason is that the Gospel is so simple, so free. In order for people to come to Christ, they have to see themselves as a sinner, with nothing to contribute to their salvation. They deserve hell, not heaven. As the verse above explains, "For there is no difference; for all have sinned and fall short of the glory of God." Regardless of how good we've been, we've not been good enough.

God justified us freely by His grace. He redeemed us or, in other words, delivered us by paying the price for our sin. By allowing His Son to take the punishment we deserved, God now has a way to pardon, not punish, the sinner. When Christ died on the cross, it was *done!* All we can do is come as an undeserving sinner and trust in Christ alone for salvation. We must agree with Christ who said on the cross, "It is finished."

As we have opportunity, we must make the Gospel clear and explain that we are accepted by God, not on the basis of Christ *plus* something we've done, but on the basis of Christ . . . *period.*

To illustrate

A man sitting in the barber's chair was using the opportunity to introduce the barber to Christ. The barber, failing to see his need for the grace of God, responded, "I'm doing the best I can."

When he finished, the man stepped out of the chair and another stepped in. The believer looked at the barber and said, "If you don't mind, I'll cut this man's hair."

The barber almost had a cardiac arrest! Immediately he responded, "You can't cut his hair. You're not a barber."

The man answered, "That's okay. I'll just do the best I can," to which the barber responded, "But your best is not good enough."

The believer explained, "And that's why you can only come to God through Christ. Your best is not good enough."

To meditate

Religion consists of two letters: d–o (do). Salvation consists of four: d–o–n–e (done!).

To pray

Thank God for the "freeness" of your salvation. Ask Him to help you develop your ability to explain the Gospel and make it clear that salvation is on the basis of Christ alone.

30

Given Anyone an Appetite Lately?

To read

> *You are the salt of the earth; but if the salt loses its flavor, how shall it be seasoned? It is then good for nothing but to be thrown out and trampled underfoot by men* (Matthew 5:13).

To consider

Salt, as it is used in Scripture, has a twofold purpose. On one hand, when applied to food, salt makes something tasty and therefore gives you an appetite for it. On the other hand, it acts as a preservative and protects something from corruption. But if salt loses that ability, it is a tasteless commodity. It is fit for nothing else than to be thrown out on the street. It is a waste of time and energy to either scatter it on the land or put it in a compost pile. As the text says, "It is then good for nothing." One commentator reports that as late as the nineteenth century in Palestine, one could see large piles of impure salt thrown out into the streets to be trampled upon.

Food does not flavor the salt; instead, the salt flavors

the food. Similarly, God wants us to give people an appetite for God and preserve righteousness on the face of the earth. Others will not give us an appetite for God and preserve righteousness. Instead, we must be the salt to them. If we fail, we are no longer serving one of the greatest purposes for which God has placed us in our neighborhood, in our school system, at our office complex, or on our jobs. Nothing helps the cause of Christ more than a believer who gives non-Christians an appetite for God. Nothing hinders the cause of Christ more than a Christian who has lost his or her ability to attract people to Christ.

To illustrate

Upon the death of a respected Christian leader, a letter addressed to him was found in his locked desk. It apparently was a letter he had shown to no one while he lived. The letter was from an individual who wrote to thank him for being the one God had used to lead the writer to the Savior.

The letter testified, "It was nothing you said that made me wish to be a Christian, it was the beauty of holiness that I saw in your very face."

To meditate

Through the message that comes from both your lips and your life, give people an appetite for God. When they come to Him, they will find the only Bread that satisfies.

To pray

Ask God to make your life a contrast to the lives of non-Christians around you. Ask Him to take out of your life what should not be there and put in what should be there.

31

No "Maybes" About It

To read

> *"Most assuredly, I say to you, he who hears My word and believes in Him who sent Me has everlasting life, and shall not come into judgment, but has passed from death into life"* (John 5:24).

To consider

Years ago, my wife and I bought a mattress for our queen-sized bed. After looking over the display, we chose the one we wanted and stepped up to the counter to make the purchase. I was surprised to learn that the mattress we purchased that night couldn't be picked up for one week. In a sense, we had it and yet we didn't have it.

As I've reflected on that, I'm so glad eternal life in Christ is not like that. Instead, the moment you trust Christ—eternal life is yours.

Look at the words used in that verse. "He who hears my Word and believes in Him who sent me—*has* everlasting life." That means right now. It is not something I pick up when I die. Then He continues, "and shall not come into judgment." That's a promise—and God never breaks promises. He concludes, "But has passed from death into life." Wow! That means death is behind me, not before me—it's past, not present or future. No wonder Paul the apostle testified that to be absent from the body is to be present with the Lord (2 Cor. 5:8).

When I came to Christ, it wasn't a "pay now and pick up later" policy. I trusted Him, and eternal life was mine. That's what I call an unbeatable deal. He's mine! I'm His! Forever!

Nobody can afford to miss out on that. Why hold back a message for others that's unlike anything they've ever heard?

To illustrate

During a war, a soldier was critically injured and the doctors were about to operate. Just before they did, one physician told the man, "It's only fair to tell you that you have one chance in one hundred of coming through this operation."

The soldier replied, "Let's get on with the operation. If I come out of it on this side, the doctors will welcome me. Should I come out of it on the other side, my Savior will welcome me."

To meditate

When we trust Christ, we are instantly and forever His because the God who cannot lie makes us a promise that cannot be broken.

To pray

Knowing the certainty of your own salvation ought to motivate you to tell someone else. Ask God to make you increasingly aware of the unchanging nature of your relationship with Christ and intensify your burden to tell others how they might enjoy that same relationship. Then expect Him to do it.

Free and Clear
Understanding and Communicating God's Offer of Eternal Love

by R. Larry Moyer

Can we state the Gospel message clearly and correctly so that non-Christians can easily grasp its meaning? This handbook will lead believers step-by-step into a thorough understanding of the Gospel and a grasp of biblical terminology and concepts. Group discussions are included for each chapter.

"I particularly benefited from the chapter 'What Then Do We Tell the Lost?' It's great to have it put so clearly."

—housewife

"In the simplest, most effective manner I've seen, Larry Moyer explains how to tell people they can know for sure they can go to heaven. . . . I highly recommend this book!"

—computer consultant

EvanTell, Inc. is an association committed to a clear presentation of the gospel through a careful study of Scripture. EvanTell's vision is to reach millions throughout the world with a clear, biblical presentation of the gospel of grace through evangelistic outreaches and the training of believers in personal evangelism and evangelistic speaking.

Do you need help overcoming your fears in evangelism and outreach, or simply knowing how to share your faith? EvanTell provides Gospel Tracts, Evangelism Training, Outreach Events, Evangelism Consulting—solutions to any need you have in evangelism and outreach. We want to help your Church, Pastor, Academic Institution, Parachurch Ministry, and you do evangelism and outreach. Sometimes evangelism is not simple, but the gospel always is! Our evangelism training and resources will help you know how to do evangelism, how to use gospel tracts and other evangelism materials, and how to witness . . . without having a nervous breakdown!

The Gospel. Clear and Simple.

P.O.Box 741417, Dallas, TX 75374

800-947-7359

e-mail: evantell@evantell.org

www.evantell.org